Mind Mapping

Step-By-Step Beginner's Guide In Creating Mind Maps!

The Blokehead

About Us

The Blokehead is an extensive series of instructional/how to books which are intended to present quick and easy to use guides for readers new to the various topics covered.

The Series is divided into the following sub-series:

1. The Blokehead Success Series

2. The Blokehead Journals

3. The Blokehead Kids Series

We enjoy and welcome any feedback to make these series even more useful and entertaining for you.

Feel free to drop us a feedback on any of these websites:

Amazon
http://amazon.com/author/theblokehead

Facebook
https://www.facebook.com/theblokehead

Get Notice of Our New Releases Here!
http://eepurl.com/5x58P

Like Us On Facebook
https://www.facebook.com/theblokehead

Table of Contents

Publisher Notes

Disclaimer

This publication is intended to provide helpful and informative material. It is not intended to diagnose, treat, cure, or prevent any health problem or condition, nor is intended to replace the advice of a physician. No action should be taken solely on the contents of this book. Always consult your physician or qualified health-care professional on any matters regarding your health and before adopting any suggestions in this book or drawing inferences from it.

Paperback Edition

Manufactured in the United States of America

Chapter 1

What is a Mind Map?

A mind map is a web-like structure composed of words, picture or images, and lines created with the sole intention of visual organization of information. A single concept or the main topic is drawn at the center of this structure, usually written on a blank landscape page. From the main topic, other major concepts are drawn out. Supporting words and ideas are loosely connected to these major concepts while minor topics are branching out until the very last idea is reached.

Mind map is said to be a type of spider diagram in Mathematics, wherein existential points are added to an Euler or a Venn diagram. Similar to a real spider, the main body of the mathematical equation (like that of the body of a spider), could spread out into other points (representing the legs of the spider). "Idea sun bursting" is another similar concept of mind map. Like the sun with its numerous rays, an idea could branch out into several smaller concepts, making it look like the actual sun.

For instance, if your central or main topic is stress, the other major concepts that could branch out from here are the definition of stress, theories and theorists of stress and the types of stress. From there, other subtopics can branch out from these major concepts such as factors causing stress, effects of stress and management of stress. Still, greater details can branch out such as relaxation techniques to combat stress and how to live a stress-free life.

Mind mapping are getting more popular as the years go by. Compared to the traditional methods of brainstorming, studying and linear note taking, mind mapping is said to be 15%-20% more effective in enhancing memory and improving learning. Many people are also acknowledging that tasks become easier and complex problems are being solved faster when mind mapping is used. This phenomenon could be attributed on how the brain works. A short review of how the brain processes the data may reveal the mystery of mind map's success. Here it is.

One of the numerous functions of the brain is that it lets you accept a flood of information that you receive from different sources. The information is stored in the knowledge bank in your brain, ready for use when you retrieve them. However, not all information received from the outside was deemed as important. Hence, only those that are considered vital are those that are retained and remembered by the brain. As for the rest of the information, they are usually lost and forgotten.

However, it is not only the level of importance of a data that would make its mark to the brain's memory bank. Other factors may include the following:

- The brain's general health. It comes without saying that the healthier the brain is, the higher the retention of information. Therefore, make it a goal to care for your brain by giving it adequate rest, stimulation and exercises and enough nutrients and oxygen. Protect it from trauma and other injury by wearing appropriate headgears when necessary.

- The number of senses used (the more senses you use, the more the retention of memory). You would notice that nursery teachers use this principle to make learning faster to the small kids. Aside from letting the children see the alphabet, for instance, they let them hear it through songs, let them touch the letters through art work or craft, let them taste the letters by asking them to bring food that begins with the letter that they are studying. College students, on the other hand, are given lectures and then some are required to undergo on-the-job-training to reinforce the learning inside the classrooms.

- The association of information to vital events or happenings in your life (this is the reason why you sometimes can remember the smallest details like what you were wearing, who you were with, what actually transpired when a very traumatic or memorable event occurred).

- The volume of information (the bigger it is, the more difficult it is to be remembered unless it is organized in a more friendly way for the brain, like mind mapping, for instance).

- Even the involvement of emotions is a factor. How you feel about a particular event would determine if that would be stored in the memory bank for good or not. Good memories are known to remain in one's memory for a long time whereas those that are deemed as bad memories are sometimes erased or deleted by the subconscious.

Mind mapping, together with these factors, could help you in various ways than you can imagine. It could be the solution that you may be seeking to improve your memory retention, expand your horizons, solve problems easily, set your goals and so much more. You could actually use it in your everyday life, both personal and professional. It is great for individual and group work. In addition, your creativity is being enhanced in the process. You actually become smarter with mind mapping. In all angles, it is a win-win situation for you when you utilize mind mapping in your life.

Chapter 2

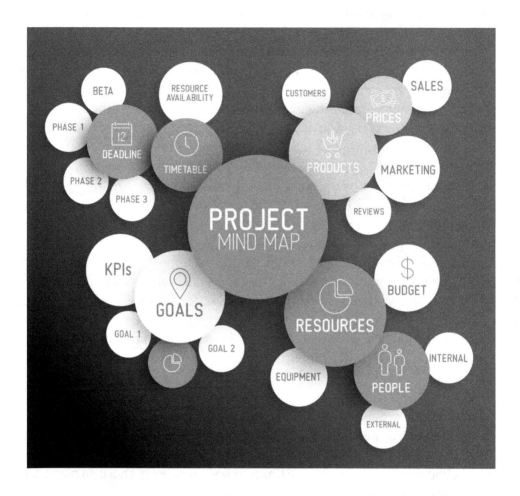

Mind Maps Advantages And Disadvantages

Mind mapping is truly increasing in popularity as more people find it more useful and effective than other methods. However, this is not to say that it is the only cure for any information related issues. Although it is true that the advantages are huge and numerous, however, just like with all things, mind mapping has its down sides, too.

Mind mapping can work wondrously for most people depending on their personality, style of learning and preference. Others find it hard though and prefer the former methods they are used to. Here are some of the advantages of mind mapping.

- The brain's creativity and potentials are being unleashed when mind maps are used since there is active stimulation of the brain cells to organize information in a visual form and not just passive encoding of data in paper or computer. Mind mapping is actually more conducive and compatible for the brain as this is the same way that the brain functions. Ideas come fast and in different areas, not in one direction and singularly only. When you do mind mapping, you are generating and releasing more ideas in a faster time since the brain has multi-processing capabilities. At the same time, the left side of the brain, the analytical side, is also not disregarded in this process. The use of words and relationships of ideas also promote active use of the left side of the brain. This is the reason why mind mapping is more effective than other methods as both sides of the brain is being utilized in the process.

- Retention of the stored memory is increased, as there is a combination of words and images compared to words alone in the conventional note-taking scheme. This visual graphical tool is said to be six times more effective in information being retained and remembered as the brain can make an imprint of the picture and store it in the memory bank for future use and reference. Moreover, the use of keywords in mind mapping to emphasize the points is found to be more effective than trying to describe or define the whole topic. Keywords are more easily retained in the memory and easier to understand and expound.

- Linking and grouping of concepts and ideas help you to organize your thoughts more accurately and more ideas are actually being generated as you dig deeper to various subtopics possible. As there is emphasis on association, the likelihood of remembering the linked points or concepts have an increased chance compared to isolated thoughts and notes.
- A mind map allows you to have a bird's view of the whole topic and its sub-topics while giving you access to the minutest detail of your topic/concept, all at a single glance. This style is friendly to users as general and specific information are readily available anytime. Moreover, seemingly complicated information is simplified as you can visualize the totality of the concept. A big plus is that it helps you focus on what is important and thus, have a greater and deeper understanding of the topic at hand.

- A lot of people appreciate the fact that with the use of mind mapping, precious time is saved as a quick glance at their notes give them all the details that they need. Unlike in the traditional way of studying, which forces them to memorize each detail separately and connect data in a much slower pace, mind mapping immediately summarizes the data that you need. In mind mapping, there is structure and the words are few, that's why memorization or processing of information is faster.

- Even when you seem to be at a loss for ideas or have reached what they call as a writer's block, mind map could get you back in the process. This systematic approach could initiate the flow of ideas as you start with the basics of why, where, what, when and how.

Indeed, there are many benefits in using mind mapping. Statistics would even support the claims of those who patronize this method, showing marked improvements in the memory and learning of those individuals. However, nothing is perfect in this world. There are also disadvantages in utilizing a mind map in your work or personal life. Here are some of them.

- Change of habit and pattern of thinking. Although change is the only constant thing in the world and yet, it is also the most resisted. For a habit to be replaced, a minimum of 21 days is needed before the new habit becomes a part of the lifestyle of an individual. For someone who is not familiar with mind mapping, acceptance of this new information-related technique would take some time. There will be resistance to the way that the data would be organized and presented. According to a study, it would require at least 12 sessions of mind mapping before a person who is resistant to this method would be able to conform to the rules of mind mapping. Why? Aside from the reality of difficulty in adapting to new things, mind mapping would also challenge your pattern of thinking. This is found to be more effective among intuitive individuals. For the logical thinkers, note taking would still be their choice as this is more compatible to their linear pattern of thinking. However, if given ample time and sessions, these individuals could learn to favor mind mapping.

- Loss of meaning. Unlike in note taking, anyone who is not present during the lecture would be able to comprehend what the topic is all about by just reading the notes. However, someone who is not part of the mind mapping session would get lost with the meaning of the map as images, symbols and keywords would be hard to decipher. Hence, mind mapping would only be beneficial to those who were actually contributors and part of the mind mapping session.

- Doing the mind map could prove challenging to others. Although it looks easy to do but a good map is actually difficult to do. It would be better if you would be able to find an instructor to teach you how to do mind map effectively. How to do the structure of the map and what are the best words and images to use are sometimes the problems being encountered by the newbies in this method. The target is not just to be able to make mind maps but to create maps that are truly helpful for learning to become faster and for information to be retained more easily.

- Misleading images and keywords. In mind mapping, there is a tendency to have a conflict with the spoken words or language versus the written map. How? For instance, during mind mapping, the participants agreed to use the keyword "vital statistics" as one of the assessment factor for a hypertensive patient. This keyword refers to the taking of blood pressure, temperature, pulse rate and respiration cycle. However, someone might mistake this for the other meaning of vital statistics (that of numbers of how many are hypertensive or the other meaning of vital statistics which is waistline, bust line and hip line). Hence, instead of being helpful during an exam, it would give the wrong answer due to wrong take of the keyword or symbol.

Mind mapping could be the ideal method to improve memory retention and enhance learning capability of some individuals but at the same time, it could be a source of confusion for those who are new to this and to those whose personalities or styles are not totally in agreement with it.

Chapter 3

Making A Mind Map

Mind mapping is designed to make information processing a lot easier for the individual who would need to study, memorize and learn the data, for what reason it may be. Tony Buzan devised the original laws or instructions for mind mapping. However, in the process of time, various modifications plus the emergence of mind map software have changed the rules on how to create a map.

Today, creating a mind map could vary according to the following:

- The purpose of the map.

- Number of person involved in mind mapping (could be an individual or group).

- Personality of the individual (organized or unstructured).

- Encoding or how to write the keywords and symbols on the map.

Here is the basic step by step guide in creating mind maps. However, variations could be made after this basic structure is done as per individual's preference and style.

1. Prepare the materials such as a clean, blank paper, preferably size A4 or larger, depending on the topic and at least three colors of pens or markers. The environment should be conducive for discussion, if with a group. Like the lighting, room temperature, table and chairs are properly installed and set. If it is an individual work, find a place where you are most comfortable, like your bedroom for instance.

2. Make a central image of the main topic on the center of the paper, with the paper on a landscape presentation. This is to prevent crowding and bumping of words and images later on as branching of the topic takes place. Why an

image instead of just writing the word of the main topic? As they say, a picture is worth a thousand words. Seeing the image could stimulate the brain to process related data on the image. Plus, this would make the activity fun and more exciting. Also, make sure that the size of the image (height and width) is around 1 to 2 inches. Do not put it in a frame as it could signal a containment of ideas for the contributors. Use three colors too, if possible. Make sure though that the guidelines on proper use of colors is observed. Colors would actually make the right cortical side of the brain more active and imaginations would be stirred up, causing more branching out of ideas and making your map more complete.

3. Start to branch out main themes or topics from the central image by doing the following:

a. Draw curved, thick and same length lines from the central image to the main themes. Why curved? Curves allow for more imaginations or ideas to flow plus they are less boring to look at. The thickness of the line would signify its importance, on the other hand. The thicker it is, the more essential it is. The same length of line is beneficial to accentuate the connection. If one line is longer, it might be taken as a separate topic and not as one of the main themes. As you are aware by now, the brain works on linkages and connections. A separated line would be taken as a different topic. Make sure all lines are therefore, connected to the central image.

b. Draw or write in printed font and all caps the names/titles of the main themes. Try to be concise when naming your main themes. Make them as single words or simple phrases, as much as possible. This would allow easy recall for the individual later on. You could also use a different colored pen for this part to signify the separation of ideas from the central theme to the main topics or themes.

4. Start to branch out into subtopics. This time the lines would be thinner to signify that it is of lesser importance compared to the main themes. Also, this time, the words can still be written in printed font but with lower cases. Again, usage of colors at this point should be done with care as you do not want to overdo it. Subtopics can be enumerated using keywords. Continue to branch out until you reach what you feel is the last idea.

5. You can add paper, if needed. After making the mind map, check it closely and see if you have covered all topics and if there is something that needs to be revised. If there are vital points, you could put them in a box so that they would stand out later and you would easily see and remember them. Use colored pens wisely. Remember, colors can aid your brain into linking and associating same ideas. Plus, it makes your brain work better as it stimulates the creative part of your mind.

Mind mapping takes several practices before it becomes easier to make and more effective as a tool for learning. Be more patient as you try to switch from a traditional method to this unique and effective method.

Chapter 4

Mind Map Elements

Compared with the elements of the traditional method of information-related processing, new users of mind mapping may feel overwhelmed with the various elements of this new method. However, to maximize the effectiveness of this method, learning about the elements and how to properly use them is a must.

The first element is color. Remember, one of the materials that you need in mind mapping is at least three pieces colored pens. Why is there emphasis in colors? From a blank page, one of the initial tasks you perform is to draw or print the central topic and to make sure that it is in color. This is because colors not only add visual interests to your map (making them attractive and fun to do) but also, they provide a wealth of meaning, which makes the information easier to remember. For instance, if your topic is love, drawing a red heart in the center would cause your brain to associate it with many things, hence making the brainstorming faster and more meaningful.

Are you also aware that colors could help your brain focus and cause more ideas to be created? A black and white picture would not cause much stimulation compared to colored ones. However, plain words would be lesser in help if your purpose were to make your creative juices flow. The best stimulator would be colored images or words.

Colors could also be used as messages in themselves. For instance, green is oftentimes associated with positive or go actions (remember the green light of traffic?). So you could use the green colored pens in your to-do action list in your map. Red, on the other hand, gives you the stop sign. When you use the color in your subtopic, for instance, foods to avoid in hypertension, emphasis on what not to take is added because of the color scheme. Lastly, colored images with words could help you retain the needed information better as intellectual prowess is increased when these two are utilized.

However, the use of colors has the tendency to be abused and misused. Adding more colors than necessary would not actually add meaning and value to your mind map. On the contrary, it might just add confusion both to you and the other contributors of the map. Take heed therefore, in using them.

The second element is icon and symbols. These little images attached to your map could mean so much than mere words alone could do. For instance, if your topic is brainstorming and your central image is a light bulb, icons such as people would depict who are the great men and women who were very good in this activity and an icon of notes (paper and pencil) could depict the great ideas that were formed.

These miniature images are actually powerful tools to help categorize your map and make it organized and more easily to be understood.
Icons and symbols are friendlier to the brain as these images could encourage other details to be formed. This would make your map more complete and comprehensive. At the same time, processing of information would be effortless as these mini-pictures could already relay the message that you want to be known.

Try to use the element of icons and symbols in all of your maps, as much as possible. You could get different icons from the internet or you could even make your own icons. As with texts, you could also add colors to your icons. For your maps to be understood and appreciated by other people, especially those non-contributors, add legends on the meaning of icons. Also, avoid overusing icons. Yes, you are encouraged to use icons in all your maps but use them wisely and appropriately.

Another element is lines. Lines are the connectors of topics. How you line your lines is of great importance. As mentioned earlier, even the thickness of the line has a meaning. There is the silent understanding that the thicker the lines, the stronger the connections of each topic to one another. This is usually used in connecting the central topic to the main themes. Broken lines, on the other hand, could mean indirect connections. In floating topics, no lines are used.

Lines could also be drawn using different colors, utilizing the principles behind the proper use of colors. Make a consistent use of colors so that in all your maps, you would be familiar in the importance of the specific color of line. For instance, every time you use green for a line, your brain would already translate it as the go or okay data while the red would be the negative and to watch out for data.

In connection to lines, boundary shapes would also fall under this element. One usually adds boundary when the topic needs to stand out from all other topics. It is therefore, incorrect that you place boundaries in all your texts as that defeats the purpose of emphasizing which is or are real important. You could use any shape for your boundaries. The lines of the boundaries could be solid or broken, depending on the content inside the boundaries. Of course, coloring the boundaries could enhance the total look plus effectiveness of the map, as long as you do not cross over the limits. Special note: If you want to share your mind map to other people, adding a floating topic with explanations on the side, could make it easily understandable for them.

Topic note is also an element in mind map. When you have a bulk of information that you want to be included in your map, use topic notes instead. This would help de-clutter your map plus it would avoid overloading the readers with information. Topic notes could be hidden from view. However, viewing them could be done in one click of a mouse. Tables, lengthy texts, charts and other information needed in the future but are not vital currently could benefit from the use of topic notes. However, when the notes are more than two pages long, attaching links would be the better option.

Another important element is images. The necessity of placing pictures or images cannot be overemphasized. Images would be equivalent to thousand words. Memory retention and stimulation of brain cells to think of various ideas could be the result of using images in your maps. As the main target is to create visual organization of data, nothing could be more helpful than an appropriate image. Plus, images make your map appear more interesting.

Lastly, the callouts are considered as part of the elements of mind map, too. When you want to draw out attention to what is really important, use callouts. What are these? These are comments that you could attach to your map so that the readers could understand the map. Samples of callouts are: "Don't forget this", "Start here", "place your feedback here" and such. Try to use callouts sparingly.

Aside from these elements, you would notice that some software could give more than fifteen elements of the mind map. However, these are the basics and most important ones.

Chapter 5

Note Taking Using Mind Maps

The traditional method of note taking is a skill to be learned. One needs practice to be able to benefit from this activity. Otherwise, you just might be writing useless information and tiring yourself in the process.

In the old method, you start with purpose in mind. Why are going to take down notes. Is it because the topic being taught would come out in the exam? Or, is it because the information being shared would be used for a term paper later on? Your purpose would determine how and what you would take note of in the lecture. For instance, one tends to be more comprehensive when the purpose is for an exam.

The subject is also another point in consideration for traditional note taking. History class would have a form of narrative style note taking while science subject would usually have bullet points style of note taking. Math subjects would have more formula and symbols rather than texts in them.

To make note taking easier, some people use short handwriting and other abbreviations. This would make you take note faster and you would have more time to understand and absorb the data being given. Afterwards, the use of colors is sometimes done when important points are highlighted using different markers. Some people use color-coding in their notes such as green marker for those priorities or important notes. Yellow markers are for important names while pink markers are for special dates. Of course, you have liberty to do your own color code. Attach legends so that other people would understand the code.

On the other hand, note taking using the new mind mapping method would require the following steps.

1. Preparedness. Be prepared in all aspects. First, secure all the materials that you would need, paper and color markers. Check the room for appropriate temperature, presence of comfortable chair and table, lighting and even,

cleanliness of the room. Make sure that there are no distractions once the activity starts. Prepare yourself physically, too. You should be comfortable and as much as possible, well-fed. If you are hungry, doing a mind map could be difficult for you. Be mentally ready. Clear your minds of other issues and concerns. Let your focus just be centered on note taking using mind mapping.

You also prepare intellectually by creating an outline of your map. This is called a pre-map. It would be to your advantage when you know the topic to be discussed. Place your central topic on the center of the paper already, with an image that suits your topic, even before the start of the lecture or discussion. You could even start coloring it. While you are at it, try to branch out some main themes so that when the actual lesson starts, you would just place the topic notes on the appropriate branches.

2. Add the topics to the central theme as soon as you hear them and recognize their category. If there were points that you cannot directly place on the branches, just make a floating topic. This simply means that the icons or text are placed outside the central topic and main themes. They are not connected to them in any way. Go back to these floating topics once the lecture or note taking activity is done. Make sure that you try to place these floating topics in their appropriate branches immediately while the linkages or associations are still fresh in your minds or else, you might not be able to remember their proper placements later on.

3. Assign powerful keywords to your map. Most of the time, you have little time to take down note in details. You would have the same information however, when correct keywords are used. You also save time when you use this technique.

4. Use appropriate color schemes. Try to organize the map by placing the same color of marker to a specific group of information.

5. After the lecture, check your map. Review, summarize and reorganize if you need to. Try to modify the map by adding images, lines, colors, boundaries, texts, icons and symbol. You do not expect the map to be perfect at this time however, you could already judge the areas where you need to improve and how you can make your map look better.

6. After the modifications and final checking, transfer the map to a clean paper. Make a mental summary of the lesson based on the mind map that you have created.

These six steps are also applicable when you are making mind maps for speeches, creating a review of a book and performing research for a book. It saves you precious time and allows you to organize your thoughts faster.

Chapter 6

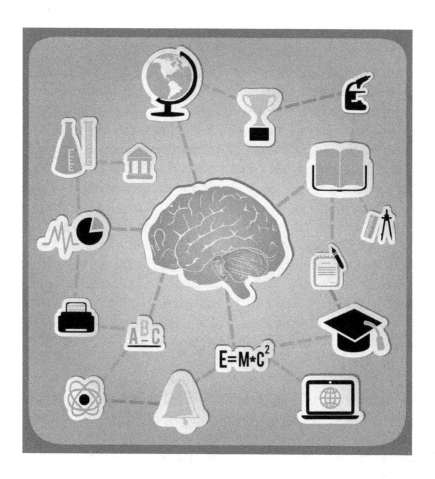

Other Uses Of Mind Maps

Unknown to many people, mind mapping is a great tool for many occasions. Here are some of them.

1. Studying. As mentioned, mind mapping is very useful in taking down notes, whether from a slide presentation or from a lecture of the professor. It summarizes vital key points in the lesson without the need to copy everything or to write down all the words of the lecturer. It organizes the lesson in such a way that when one glances at the map, the totality of the lesson is at hand. It cooperates with the brain so that studying the lesson is easier and

retention of information to the memory is more effective and lasting. Another advantage of using mind mapping when studying is when examinations are at hand. Studying these maps to review the lessons learned make your learning simpler and efforts are lesser. At the same time, you could even connect all the lessons just by simply arranging the maps according to the timeframe and topics of the lessons. Statistics has shown how the performance and grades of those students who utilized mind maps have increased over time.

2. Writing. Whether you are a professional or just an amateur writer, mind mapping could be your best friend. Many writers have difficulties arranging the information in such a way that the readers would be able to comprehend what they want to convey in a snap. Sometimes, the overload of information crowd the script and instead of helping the readers understand the key points, they become lost in the complexity of the article. Mind mapping could eliminate unnecessary data and at the same time, create a flow that would be friendly to the readers. This is due to the organization of the piled data. Another big plus of mind mapping is when the writers are experiencing the so-called "writer's block". This is the temporary condition in which the writer has difficulties in proceeding with writing or worse, the writer has inability to write down anything at all. With mind mapping, this condition is eliminated or lessened as the brain is usually stimulated to come out with various ideas with the use of images, topic notes, colors, lines, icons and symbols. Studies revealed that even the use of a single photo is effective enough to draw out hundreds of ideas, in one sitting alone.

3. Giving presentations or speeches. A skilled presenter or speaker has one goal in mind, that is, to be able to transfer the information that he or she has to the audience, in such a way that they would come out of the lecture with full comprehension of the lesson or presentation. This is a challenging task, indeed. Mind map could help you with this by organizing the information in such a way that the flow of thoughts would be easy for the audience to grasp. With the allotted time you are given to discuss, mind maps could show you the important topics that you need to focus on and to avoid unnecessary majoring on minor details. Sometimes, it is not about how lengthy or compact the lesson is but on how you were able to put emphasis on the important details that matter. At the end of the presentation, did the audience actually learn something? Did you have an organized speech or were your points scattered?

4. Problem solving. A wonderful way to remedy a problem is thru mind mapping. The most effective method so far is by using the 5W and H style. How is this done? For instance, your concern is how to save money. Draw an image

in the very center of the paper – perhaps a bundle of bills. Color it and have six same length lines from the drawing going outwardly. On the first line or main theme is what. Under that category, list down the amount you want to have, the items that you want to have savings on (like time, energy or credit card expenditures). On the other branch, who, you could list down the names of the people, whom you think would be able to help you. You could make another sub-branch from that branch and write down the names of the people you need to avoid in order to be able to save. Also, under who, you could take note of who you would like to emulate. Then follow suit with the why until you reach the how. These are just samples. You could make your own branches depending on your problem. Mind mapping could give you a bird's view of the real problem and the probable solutions. At the same time, logical and creative solutions could be drawn out from these mind maps as both sides of the brain are being stimulated to function. A lot of office executives have attested to the fact how mind mapping has helped them greatly in their quests to find solutions for their problems. Some have attributed 30% of successful problems solved by using the method of mind mapping.

5. Project Management. Very similar to problem solving, mind mapping is also great for managing small to medium projects. Instead o the 5W and the H, the focus of the map would center on the budget, resources, scope, people and deadline of the project. From there, you could make branches out for every point. As you go through the project, you could use the mind map to see if the plan is working. If there are problems encountered on the process of completing the project, mind mapping could also identify the steps to be taken to remedy the problem. Then proceed with the original map to continue with the project.

6. Decision-making skill. One of the hardest things to do is to make a sound decision. However, this task is made easier, thanks to mind mapping. With this method, all the cards are presented on the table. All possible actions to be taken are considered. All vital points are included. All the options are listed down. Visualizing the solution and the possible outcome is the main difference why mind mapping is a great tool to use to make a decision.

7. Brainstorming. Simply listing down all the suggested ideas during brainstorming session might not be helpful in coming out with great solutions or answers. However, with mind mapping, all those suggested ideas could be placed in categories. In this way, unrelated ideas could be placed in a floating topic, and they would not get in the way of more meaningful and useful ideas. Mind mapping also allow for structuring of these ideas into meaningful con-

cepts rather than having them loosely scattered everywhere. Ideas that can be used in the future could be stored instead of disregarded.

8. Goal setting. Maybe you have heard it a dozen of times "When you fail to plan, you plan to fail". Therefore, you are aware of how important it is to set goals. However, many people find this tedious. Not so with mind mapping. As areas are categorized, you would be able to set goals in every aspect of your life and in a fun way, too. Also, there is more possibility of these plans coming to fulfillment as the brain is not only aware of the plan but it has a mental picture of the plan. Another famous quote to use is "what the mind can conceive, the body can achieve". In this quote, mental vision is very important for the achievement of the plan.

9. Learning a new language. Another difficult task that is made easy by mind mapping is the learning of a new language. If you would just go run into learning a language without organizing the learning plan, you are bound to encounter difficulties. However, when the goals are set and when the steps and plan of actions are well-written and organized, the adaptation of the new language becomes easy.

10. Getting things done. Yes, paper and pen is also an effective way of accomplishing your to-do list. However, mind mapping is also another way to ensure that your activities are done correctly and on time. Visualizing and writing down the activities can provide the focus you need to prioritize correctly your activities. Plus, the map could provide you added information on how to tackle the activities in the most efficient way.

There are other uses of mind mapping that could prove very beneficial whether in your personal or professional life. Take advantage of these uses and see yourself progress in your walk towards success and victory.

Chapter 7

Mind Mapping For Kids

One is never too young to start training for mind mapping. Actually, the best person to teach this wonderful method is among the young population. Why is this so? Remember that kids tend to use the right side of their brains more often. They are highly imaginative and very creative. Adults, on the other hand, tend to utilize the left side of the brain more often. They are more logical, practical and analytical.

Mind mapping encourages the use of both sides of the brain. Imagine what could be achieved when this is done. Children would enjoy attending schools more. They would learn more easily, too. Plus, their problem solving and decision-making skills would be developed and enhanced even at a very young age. You could expect to have more responsible adults when these kids grow up. It would be truly an advantage when children know how to practice mind mapping as early as they can. Here are some pointers on how you could teach mind mapping to young children.

First, you do not actually "teach" mind mapping to them. You let them discover and practice the method by themselves. You would take the role of a coach. You guide them on how to use mind mapping in any situation that they are in. You can do this in your everyday routine. For instance, do this during story telling time. Get them a blank page and while you are telling them a story, ask them to draw as creatively as possible. Make your words very descriptive so that there is enough room for the kids' imagination to run.

After the story telling and drawing, you could evaluate if the activity is a success. Ask your child to tell the story back using the drawing. Supposedly, the sketches made would make him/her remember the full story and use those as guides in his/her storytelling. Just repeat the process until the child adapts the method. When you see your child progressing into this activity, make it more challenging by him/her starting the storytelling itself (using a new story, of course) plus making his/her own drawing and re-telling of the story afterwards.

You would be amazed at how creative children are and how very good their memories are. Another very important thing to remember while you are coaching your child into mind mapping is to make this activity fun. Do not become the overbearing and strict coach or else, the children would be resistant to this activity. Learning should be enjoyable.

Make learning fun by looking into details on how to make it fun for the child. Make the room or the area conducive for thinking. Make sure that the child is comfortable, not hungry, sleepy or tired. Let the child choose the colors that he/she prefers. Guide the child and not force him or her into doing mind mapping. Leave room for mistakes. Remember, learning is a process. It does not occur in one sitting only. Be appreciative of the child's progress, no matter how small it may seem.

Consistency is also a must. Try to incorporate this activity whenever you can. For instance, instead of just planning your kid's birthday party on your own, why don't you involve him or her and let them make decisions regarding the party. Get a clean sheet of paper and place a drawing of your child in the center with a cake or balloon. Use the 5W and H method. Ask your child to draw out 6 lines (this depends on the child's age and capability). From who to invite, to other details of the party, include the child in enumerating ideas regarding the party.

As the child grows, make the mind mapping activities more challenging and appropriate for age. In the child's studies, always try to incorporate mind mapping so that the learning process and information related activities would be improved. This would become a part of child's lifestyle and mind mapping would be automatic for him or her when the child grows up into adulthood.

Chapter 8

Other Considerations In Using Mind Mapping

Another plus factor in using mind mapping is that you also improve in other areas of your life, like in the following: Discipline, Listening and Speed Reading. Why? An effective map would require that you also enhance these skills so that you could do mind mapping effortlessly.

For one to become a great mind mapper, one needs to practice consistently. Discipline is needed in this area. The ideal way to start is through simple cases where mind mapping can be done. Try to practice as much as you can. As you learned earlier, it would need at least 12 mind mapping sessions before it becomes part of your lifestyle.

One good tip while you are practicing is that you do it right from the very start. Practice right so that you can perfect it right. This would indeed require discipline on your part because sometimes, it could get frustrating. Even though it would take more time before you finally get the hang of it, be patient. The rewards are well-worth your efforts in the long run.

Another consideration to take is the importance of boosting your listening skill. Mind mapping is oftentimes used during lessons and brainstorming. Learn the art of active listening. Most often than not, selective listening occurs. This is hearing only the things that you want to hear and missing out on the other things that the speaker is trying to convey to you. If you continue in this practice, your map would be missing so many areas. Many ideas would not be included. You would defeat the purpose of trying to gather all pertinent information and organizing them in such a way that your brain could visualize and achieve them.

When you are doing active listening, remove all other things that are crowding your mind. Focus on the task at hand. Look intently at the speaker. Pay attention and give the speaker your undivided attention. Listen with your ears and your heart. Clarify some things if you missed hearing them. Ask valid questions. Also, provide feedback whenever possible.

Communication is a two-way process. Plus, non-verbal communication, such as body language, facial expressions and social distance also send messages as loud as verbal language to the other person. Therefore, put great care also on these things. Make sure that your words and body actions jive with the message that you want to send.

Lastly, speed-reading skill would be of great advantage to your mind-mapping endeavor. As you know, mind mapping could also be used for knowledge management, summarizing books and other activities requiring the need to speed-read. However, speed-reading is not the main target alone. Make sure that comprehension is very much intact while the speed in reading is improved.

Here are some tips on how to develop the skill of speed-reading.

1. Find a place conducive for reading. The number one priority is good lighting. Make sure that the room is well lit. Also, make sure that the place is free from any distractions or noises. Even if you are used to having music when you are reading, your speed in reading would greatly improve when there are no unnecessary noises. Remove cellphones, turn off television or radio, and place a "do not disturb" sign at the door. If it is impossible to have total solitude, use earplugs to minimize the noise. Lastly, try not to read in bed. It has been discovered that this would cause you to be sleepy.

2. Read with your eyes and not with your lips. Using your lips could slow you down even if there are no sounds coming out of it. To stop this habit, you could hold a finger against your mouth when you are reading. Eventually, this habit would be removed from you.

3. Try to understand a group of words. This is faster than trying to comprehend single words each time you read. You could do this by trying to hold the book back farther than you used to do. By doing so, you take in more words at once. Train yourself to understand group of words every time you read. Get the gist of the article while you comprehend the message.

4. Avoid re-reading lines. Train yourself to avoid going back to previously read lines. This is a great time waster. Make sure that you have understood the context the first time you read it.

5. Read when you are most alert. This is highly individualized. Some people find morning as the best time to do the important things as they function well

during this time. For some, it would be nighttime. Start also reading the most important article as your brain is most active at this time. This is so that you would have greater comprehension to the more important things of the articles.

6. Speed-reading is not just about speed, as already mentioned. You could allow for some slow reading time when the passage of the article seems difficult to understand. Do the opposite when the text is something that you are already familiar with. Try to do your best speed when the topic is something that you are already aware of.

7. You could also get the gist of the whole passage by reading the titles and subtitles. Also, you would have an idea of the totality of the article by reading the introduction and the conclusion first. The body usually contains the supporting details of the introduction and the conclusion.

8. Lastly, time yourself. You could see how much progress you are having by doing so.

These three qualities, being disciplined, speed-reading and having active listening skill could help make your mind mapping easier. You would be surprised how quick you would be able to draw out a map and organize your thoughts. As you practice mind mapping in every area of your life, you would discover the total effects it would have on you, both personally and professionally. Do mind mapping now and enjoy its benefits today!

Yap Kee Chong
8345 NW 66 ST #B7885
Miami, FL 33166

Copyright 2015

Get Notice of Our New Releases Here!
http://eepurl.com/5x58P

Check Out Our Other Books

Self Help

ADHD Adult: How To Recognize & Cope With Adult ADHD In 30 Easy Steps

Conversation Skills: How To Talk To Anyone & Build Quick Rapport In 30 Steps

Ending Emotional Eating: Tips And Strategies To Stop Emotional Eating In 30 Days

House Cleaning Guide: 70+ Top Natural House Cleaning Hacks Exposed

Intuitive Eating: 30 Intuitive Eating Tips & Strategies For A Healthy Body & Mind Today!

Organized Mind: How To Excel In Math & Science In 30 Easy Steps

Organized Mind: How To Rewire Your Brain To Stop Bad Habits & Addiction In 30 Easy Steps

Organized Mind: How To Think Straight And Make All The Right Life Decisions In 30 Easy Steps

Stress Eating: How to Handle the Stress Triggers that Lead to Emotional Eating, Stress Eating and Binge Eating & Beat It Now!

Creative Confidence: How To Unleash Your Confidence & Easily Write 3000 Words Without Writer's Block Box Set

Creative Confidence: How To Unleash Your Confidence, Be Super Innovative & Design Your Life In 30 Days

Journaling: The Super Easy Five Minute Journaling Like A Pro Box Set

Journaling: The Super Easy Five Minute Basics To Journaling Like A Pro In 30 Days

397 Journaling Writing Prompts & Ideas: Your Secret Checklist To Journaling Like A Super Pro In Five Minutes

Habit Stacking: How To Set Smart Goals & Avoid Procrastination In 30 Easy Steps (Box Set)

Habit Stacking: Goal Setting: How To Set Smart Goals & Achieve All Of Them Now

Habit Stacking: How To Change Any Habit In 30 Days

Habit Stacking: How To Beat Procrastination In 30+ Easy Steps (The Power Habit Of A Go Getter)

Habit Stacking: How To Write 3000 Words & Avoid Writer's Block (The Power Habits Of A Great Writer)

Declutter Your Home Fast: Organization Ideas To Declutter & Organize Your Home In Just 15 Minutes A Day!

Emotional Vampires: How to Deal with Emotional Vampires & Break the Cycle of Manipulation. A Self Guide to Take Control of Your Life & Emotional Freedom

Memory Improvement: Techniques, Tricks & Exercises How To Train and Develop Your Brain In 30 Days

Mind Mapping: Step-By-Step Beginner's Guide In Creating Mind Maps!

Hobbies & Crafts

Doodling: How To Master Doodling In 6 Easy Steps

Making Costume Jewelry: An Easy & Complete Step By Step Guide
Paracord Bracelets & Projects: A Beginners Guide (Mastering Paracord Bracelets & Projects Now)

Jewelry Making For Beginners: A Complete & Easy Step by Step Guide
How To Make Jewelry With Beads: An Easy & Complete Step By Step Guide

Silver Jewelry Making: An Easy & Complete Step by Step Guide
Gaming & Entertainment

The Miner's Combat Handbook: 50+ Unofficial Minecraft Strategies For Combat Handbook Exposed

The Miner's Traps: 50+ Unofficial Minecraft Traps Exposed!

The Miner's XBOX 360 Handbook: 50+ Unofficial Minecraft XBOX 360 Tips & Tricks Exposed!

Miner's Kids Stories: Unofficial 2015 Box Set of 50+ Minecraft Short Stories, Jokes, Memes & More For Kids

Miner's Survival Handbook: Unofficial 2015 Box Set of Minecraft Cheats, Seeds, Redstone, Mods, House And More!

The Miner's Redstone 2015: Top Unofficial Minecraft Redstone Handbook Exposed!

The Miner's Seeds 2015: Top Unofficial Minecraft Seeds Tips & Tricks Handbook Exposed!

The Miner's Mod 2015 : Top Unofficial Minecraft Mods Tips & Tricks Handbook Exposed!

The Miner's Pocket Edition 2015: Top Unofficial Tips & Tricks Minecraft Handbook Exposed!

The Miner's Jokes For Kids : 50+ Unofficial Collection Of Minecraft Fun Jokes, Memes, Puns, Riddles & More!

The Miner's Craft 2015: Top Unofficial Minecraft Tips & Tricks Handbook Exposed!

The Miner's House 2015: Top Unofficial Minecraft House Tips & Handbook Exposed!

The Miner's A - Z Unofficial Compendium For Minecraft Combat Success
Kids Stories From The Miner: 50+ Unofficial Collection Of Fun Minecraft Stories Of Creepers, Skeleton & More For Kids

The Miner's Cheats 2015: Top Unofficial Minecraft Cheats Handbook Exposed!

Poker Strategy: How To Get The Unfair Winning Edge In Any Tournament. The Secret Strategies Of Poker Mega Stars Revealed!

Diet

10 Day Green Smoothie Cleanse: A Box Set of 100+ Recipes For A Healthier You Now!

10 Day Green Smoothie Cleanse: 50 New And Fat Burning Paleo Smoothie Recipes For Your Rapid Weight Loss Now

10 Day Green Smoothie Cleanse: 50 New Beauty Blast Recipes To A Sexy New You Now

10 Day Green Smoothie Cleanse: 50 New Cholesterol Crusher Recipes To Reduce Cholesterol The Natural Way

10 Day Green Smoothie Cleanse: 50 New Cholesterol Crusher Recipes To Reduce Cholesterol The Natural Way

10 Day Green Smoothie Cleanse: 50 New Sleep Helper Recipes Revealed! Get The Sleep You Deserved Now

Autoimmune Paleo Cookbook: Top 30 Autoimmune Paleo (AIP) Breakfast Recipes Revealed!

Dash Diet Plan: The Ultimate Dash Diet Cheat Sheet For Weight Loss

Dash Diet Recipes: Top DASH Diet Cookbook & Eating Plan For Weight Loss

Green Smoothie Weight Loss: 70 Green Smoothie Recipes For Diet, Quick Detox, Cleanse & To Lose Weight Now!

Paleo Diet For Beginners: Top 30 Paleo Snack Recipes Revealed!

Paleo Diet For Beginners: Top 40 Paleo Lunch Recipes Revealed!
Paleo Diet For Beginners: Top 30 Paleo Cookie Recipes Revealed!

Paleo Diet For Beginners: Top 30 Paleo Comfort Food Recipes Revealed!

Paleo Diet For Beginners: Top 30 Paleo Bread Recipes Revealed!

Paleo Diet For Beginners: 70 Top Paleo Diet For Athletes Exposed!

Paleo Diet For Beginners: Top 30 Paleo Pasta Recipes Revealed!

Paleo Diet For Beginners: Top 50 Paleo Smoothie Recipes Revealed!

Autoimmune Paleo Cookbook: Top 30 Autoimmune Paleo Recipes Revealed!

Paleo Diet For Beginners: A Box Set Of 100+ Gluten Free Recipes For A Healthier You Now!

Super Immunity Superfoods: Super Immunity Superfoods That Will Boost Your Body's Defences & Detox Your Body For Better Health Today!

The DASH Diet Box Set: A Collection of Dash Diet Recipes & Cheat Sheets Health

Borderline Personality Disorder: 30+ Secrets How To Take Back Your Life When Dealing With BPD (A Self Help Guide)

Ebola Outbreak Survival Guide 2015: 5 Key Things You Need To Know About The Ebola Pandemic & Top 3 Preppers Survival Techniques They Don't Want You To Know

Thyroid Diet: Thyroid Solution Diet & Natural Treatment Book For Thyroid Problems & Hypothyroidism Revealed!

Bipolar Disorder: Am I Bipolar? How Bipolar Quiz & Tests Reveal The Answers

Bipolar Diet: How To Create The Right Bipolar Diet & Nutrition Plan- 4 Easy Steps Reveal How!

Bipolar Type 2: Creating The RIGHT Bipolar Diet & Nutritional Plan

Bipolar 2: Bipolar Survival Guide For Bipolar Type II: Are You At Risk? 9 Simple Tips To Deal With Bipolar Type II Today

Bipolar Teen: Bipolar Survival Guide For Teens: Is Your Teen At Risk? 15 Ways To Help & Cope With Your Bipolar Teen Today

Bipolar Child: Bipolar Survival Guide For Children: 7 Strategies To Help Your Children Cope With Bipolar Today

Anxiety and Depression: Stop!-Top Secrets To Beating Depression & Coping With Anxiety... Revealed! - Exclusive Edition

Anxiety And Phobia Workbook: 7 Self Help Ways How You Can Cure Them Now

7 Top Anxiety Management Techniques: How You Can Stop Anxiety And Release Stress Today

Depression Help: Stop! – 5 Top Secrets To Create A Depression Free Life… Finally Revealed – Exclusive Edition

Anxiety Workbook: Top 10 Powerful Steps How To Stop Your Anxiety Now... - Exclusive Edition

Depression Cure: The Depression Cure Formula: 7 Steps To Beat Depression Naturally Now – Exclusive Edition

Depression Workbook: A Complete & Quick 10 Steps Program To Beat Depression Now

Depression Self Help: 7 Quick Techniques To Stop Depression Today!
Hormone Balance: How To Reclaim Hormone Balance, Sex Drive, Sleep & Lose Weight Now

Fitness

Kettlebell: How To Perform Simple High Level Kettlebell Sculpting Moves Top 30 Express Kettlebell Workout Revealed!

Strength Training Diet & Nutrition: 7 Key Things To Create The Right Strength Training Diet Plan For You

Strength Training Machine: How To Stay Motivated At Strength Training With & Without A Strength Training Machine

Strength Training For Seniors: An Easy & Complete Step By Step Guide For You

Strength Training For Runners: The Best Forms Of Weight Training For Runners

Strength Training For Beginners: A Start Up Guide To Getting In Shape Easily Now!

The Ultimate Body Weight Workout: 50+ Advanced Body Weight Strength Training Exercises Exposed (Book One)

The Ultimate Body Weight Workout: 50+ Body Weight Strength Training For Women

The Ultimate Body Weight Workout: Top 10 Essential Body Weight Strength Training Equipments You MUST Have NOW

The Ultimate Body Weight Workout: Transform Your Body Using Your Own Body Weight

Survival & Outdoors

Preppers Guide: The Essential Prepper's Guide Box Set

Preppers Guide: The Essential Prepper's Guide & Handbook For Survival!
Self-Sufficiency: A Complete Guide For Family's Preparedness And Survival!

Bushcraft: 101 Bushcraft Survival Skill Box Set

Bushcraft: The Ultimate Bushcraft 101 Guide To Survive In The Wilderness Like A Pro

Bushcraft: 7 Top Tips Of Bushcraft Skills For Beginners

Religion

Religion For Atheists: The Ultimate Atheist Guide & Manual On The Religion Without God

Finance

Bitcoin: The Ultimate A-Z Of Profitable Bitcoin Trading & Mining Guide Exposed!

Minimalist: How To Prepare & Control Your Minimalist Budget In 30 Days Or Less & Get
More Money Out Of Life Now

Cooking & Recipes

Kids Recipes Book: 70 Of The Best Ever Lunch Recipes That All Kids Will Eat… Revealed!

Kids Recipes Book: 70 Of The Best Ever Dinner Recipes That All Kids Will Eat… Revealed!

Kids Recipes: 70 Of The Best Ever Big Book Of Recipes That All Kids Love… Revealed!

Kids Recipes Books: 70 Of The Best Ever Breakfast Recipes That All Kids Will Eat…
Revealed!

Barbecue Cookbook: 70 Time Tested Barbecue Meat Recipes Revealed!
Vegetarian Cookbooks: 70 Complete Vegan Recipes For Her Weight Loss & Diet Guide…
Revealed!

Vegan Cookbook: 70 Vegan Breakfast Diet For Her Weight Loss Book… Revealed!

Vegan Cookbooks: 70 Scrumptious Vegan Dinner Recipes For Her Weight Loss… Revealed!

Vegan Cookbooks: 70 Vegan Lunch Recipes & Vegan Diet For Her Weight Loss Guide
Revealed!

Barbecue Cookbook: 140 Of The Best Ever Barbecue Meat & BBQ Fish Recipes Book... Revealed!

BBQ Recipe: 70 Of The Best Ever Barbecue Vegetarian Recipes... Revealed!

BBQ Cookbooks: Make Your Summer Go With A Bang! A Simple Guide To Barbecuing

Barbecue Recipes: 70 Of The Best Ever Barbecue Fish Recipes... Revealed!
BBQ Recipe Book: 70 Of The Best Ever Healthy Barbecue Recipes... Revealed!

Barbecue Cookbook: 140 Of The Best Ever Healthy Vegetarian Barbecue Recipes Book... Revealed!

Grain Free Cookbook: Top 30 Brain Healthy, Grain & Gluten Free Recipes Exposed!

Technology

Scrum – Ultimate Guide To Scrum Agile Essential Practices!
Raspberry Pi: Raspberry Pi Guide On Python & Projects Programming In Easy Steps

Languages

Learn Languages: How To Learn Any Language Fast In Just 168 Hours (7 Days)

Pets

Essential Oils For Cats: Essential Oil Recipes, Usage, And Safety For Your Cat

Sports

Golf Instruction: How To Break 90 Consistently In 3 Easy Steps

CPSIA information can be obtained
at www.ICGtesting.com
Printed in the USA
LVHW080944130321
681456LV00023B/199